fallibility

Many Voices Project

fallibility

Elizabeth Oness

First Edition
Library of Congress Control Number: 2008934508
ISBN: 978-0-89823-244-8
MVP Number 118
Cover design and interior book by Erin Malkowski
Author photograph by Joel Ianuzzi

The publication of *fallibility* is made possible by the generous support of
the Jerome Foundation and other contributors to New Rivers Press.

For academic permission please contact Frederick T. Courtright at
570-839-7477 or permdude@eclipse.net. For all other permissions,
contact The Copyright Clearance Center at 978-750-8400 or info@copyright.com.

New Rivers Press is a nonprofit literary press associated with
Minnesota State University Moorhead.

Wayne Gudmundson, Director
Alan Davis, Senior Editor
Donna Carlson, Managing Editor
Allen Sheets, Art Director
Thom Tammaro, Poetry Editor
Kevin Carollo, MVP Poetry Coordinator
Liz Severn, MVP Fiction Coordinator
Frances Zimmerman, Business Manager
        Publishing Interns: Samantha Jones, Andrew Olson, Mary Huyck Mulka
        fallibility Book Team: Mary Huyck Mulka, Nathan Logan
        Editorial Interns: Michael Beeman, Mary Huyck Mulka, Nathan Logan,
                Kayla Lundgren, Tarver Mathison, Amber Olds,
                Jessica Riepe, Alyssa Schafer, Andrea Vasquez
        Design Interns: Alex Ehlen, Andrew Kerr, Erin Malkowski,
                Megan McCleary, Lindsay Stokes

Printed in the United States of America.

New Rivers Press
c/o MSUM
1104 7th Avenue South
Moorhead, MN 56563
www.newriverspress.com

For Chad ~
again, and always

Table of Contents

I

Belleek

I am troubled, I'm dissatisfied, I'm Irish.

For years I resisted it, the only
shatterable part of my inheritance—

china sprinkled with insipid shamrocks,
two tones of green, the sweetly clustered leaves

bordering the plates in an Irish ring-a-rosy,
unfurling from the teapot's stalk

like a fairy invention, a porcelain version of
a time that never was.

There was no blarney in the house where I grew up.
We were tight-lipped, silent;
                              superfluity was sin.

Nothing to do? I'll give you something to do.
You want something to cry about? I'll give you something ...

My grandmother cried leaving Ireland the last time.
I sat beside her on the plane

staring down at the Cliffs of Moher,
water breaking over the wrack-mired stone.

She had shown me the house where she grew up,
the nettled fields, the barn

where her father locked her in a stall
and she stayed all night afraid.

A vine of angry fathers, mothers porcelain pale.

When I left my father's house,
I too knew it would be my final visit.

But I left without tears, shook the dust from my feet,
the only nostalgia a wordless music.

I was as guilty as anyone. I knew it.

Every time I opened my mouth there was drama,
accusation, but my words fell on whiskey

dissolved in that distillate warmth.

And still this problem with the china—
unadorned it would be lovely,

translucent weave of white on white,
the palest gloss of yellow

tipped inside the teapot's stem.
It's the sentiment that spoils it,

as if the unembellished can't be pleasing.
I want a teapot bearing

each denial of the body, bitterness and bad teeth.

But even the blemished past isn't
                              unembellished truth.

The darker truth
is what's confided. Her whisper

whispers through me now: *Come here little one....*
Come here 'til I tell you.

The Warmth of Blue Glass

I come back to Pocantico to see Chagall's windows,
disruptive angels swirling around me
contained in rectangles of variate light.
Twenty years ago, on a grade-school trip,
an old woman in sturdy shoes lectured
on the prophets suspended in glass. I saw
whorls of yellow rolling through violet,
faces submerged in blue—not like
my church, where saints wore robes
that fell in perfect pleats, where I learned
I was overseen, charted. God saw every
imperfect impulse. I remember the drone of Mass
in Latin, meanings I couldn't know,
like the elusive language of adults, hovering
above me like a web I would rise to tangle in.
In late afternoon the chapel is empty;
the angels sink into curls of darkness.
Chagall painted on glass after piecing it together,
etching faces into buoyant fragments, swelling
the leaded borders with wind. His lines
tickle every static image of God,
swirl the last daylight over patterns in stone.

Water That Feeds the Battenkill River

We had to be quiet; noise
would scare the fish away.
My line ran out, invisible in shade,

bright where sun leaked through
and touched it. In my hands
the winding draw of the stream,

then an angry body pulled
against my arms, pulled against
the pivoting current.

Out of water, it flapped
and shimmered in the air,
but my fingers weren't brave enough

to grasp what I'd caught,
and my father twisted the barb
from its mouth. I watched

the heaving gills, useless
in the humid air, imagined water
rushing in behind my cheeks.

A silvered rainbow beat
behind the bloodied gills,
pale red, green, shifting under light.

My father wanted a photo—
my finger slipped inside a gill,
but I didn't want to feel

the inside of its stiffened mouth.
Watching my father's knife
make its quick line down the belly,

I wondered if he wished
for sons
instead of daughters.

The Cost

The picture in *The Children's Bible* showed
the fullness of God's test: Abraham,
his upraised hand, knife poised against

a bilious sky. His sandals planted
in the dust—the human digging in
against what God requires. He stood

above his son in the neatly painted clearing,
boulders and stones pleasingly arranged,
while Isaac, helpless on his back, diapered

like a baby, waited on a pyre of branches,
ready for the flames. The church hall
where we went each Sunday

a Catholic school gymnasium filled with
folding chairs. Behind the wooden altar,
curtains over cinderblock painted sullen green.

Babies wailed above the murmured Mass
and their wordless protestation
confirmed what I believed—

that every Sunday after church
the priest would choose a child
to offer up to God.

The camel through the needle's eye,
the narrow path, it seemed so clear:
there was God's way or mine.

Skin pricked by wool, fidgeting,
there seemed little choice—
the path would be my own pleasure,

my own sweet darkness.
I would believe in other stories
and there would be a cost.

The Discovery of Wine

The story before the stories we know
the hours hurrying toward the sun, the emergent
phase already inscribed, the body become a vine,
the vine bearing grapes, and from the fruit of
youthful beauty, watered by the god who would not
weep, the sweet red grapes inviting touch
and Dionysus took them in his hand and crushed
them in his fingers and on his tongue the sweetness
hummed, the unexpected red caress, a boy
transformed into the vine and fruit, his spirit become
spirits, in this other form the pleasure he inspired
would lift away all pain, cause a dizzying
forgetfulness to anyone who took him in.

Elegy

Unexpected, it wings the smallest spears
so lightly, the touch of cold like the touch
of a new hand, which asks the tentative body
to ache into a flowering that leaves the earth behind.
This is the season of darkness increasing,
of silence pressed against the panes. This is the first
bright chill of morning, the heat not yet turned on,
there is no refuge. There is only sunlight
silvered in pale tufts of grass,
this stinging alive in a season's turning,
like the moment after the news of your death,
when the flame-leafed tree outside my door
grew distinct in a terrible clarity,
the way some things are most
bright before their passing.

The Silver Screen

The photos in their silver frames watch over us.

An eight-by-ten glossy, taken in Atlanta—
the opening night of *Gone with the Wind*.

The grandfather I had never met, elegant in a top hat.
My grandmother in furs, smiling from an unfamiliar face;

she liked to talk about the people that she knew,
how Clark Gable came to dinner.

When I was small I'd visit her dark apartment,
fake fire in the lobby grate.

In the polished wooden elevator,
the diamond window filled with light and dark.

When my uncle came, martinis at noon.
She'd pour his second drink—

Two wings to fly on! She'd laugh and click her teeth.

Lunch was always the same—roast lamb with mint jelly,
mashed potatoes, string beans and soft onion rye.

I dug hollows in the potatoes, put butter in
and covered it, then slipped into the warm yellow.

A portrait of my mother hung in the hall. She looked
so perfectly finished.

My mother buttons every button to the top.

My grandmother's hand was mutilated: half a nubble thumb,
two of her fingers shortened and skinny,

like chicken bones covered with skin.
My mother wouldn't tell me how it got like that.

In the bathroom and the bedroom there are pills
on silver trays. Jars of cream with silver lids.

All sealed tight, neatly in a row.

She called herself a *Hoosier girl*, dancing to New York—
vaudeville her escape. She silvered some secret

with brash stories of her past. The first time
my grandfather asked to see her home—

Mister, she said, *I know my way home*,
and she cackled when she told me,

I was fresh as paint!

She'd take me to the Gold Lake Dairy,
buy *The Racing Form, The Enquirer, Catholic New York*.

She tapped her nubbled stub against
the tabloid pictures: Caroline Kennedy—

no bra—shameful how her nipples showed.

Her apartment filled with figurines and books.
She read "to keep up" my mother said.

My mother wraps her mother's secrets
around her like a shroud. Mysterious then

the books I was bequeathed: Marianne Moore's poems,
Yeats' *A Vision* with notecards tucked inside—

Reference to Countess Cathleen. Symbolism.

Walter Pater—Father of Symbolism?
Mother: A Cloudy Goddess—

For My Father, on My Sister's Wedding Day

My father sits at the kitchen table,
lower lip thrust out, pretending to read
The New York Times, pretending not to be excited.
Early this morning the sky was opaque,
but the clouds unlocked themselves,
shivered apart, letting the cold spring sun
speckle the lawn. I once believed
his predictions for sun or rain were sure knowledge.
The muffled hum of a blowdryer and my sisters'
laughter seeps down through the walls from upstairs.
I sit with him at the kitchen table,
drinking coffee, reading the paper;
the mirrors of the house are filled
with daughters. In a window's reflection
he straightens his tie. I smile at his shadow
in the glass and look out over
the April yard coming green.
At the bottom of the slope is the brick springhouse
set in the curve of the grass and gravel drive.
When I was small he took me inside
to see where faucet water came from.
Inside, the air was cool and still;
we stood on the cement ledge, looking into
the gray silence of deep water,
dark surface invisible.

Labor

In spring he pulled the siding down
like feathers from the frame.
He opened the barn's south face,
dismantled the sagging doors,
letting sunlight penetrate the unlit quiet,
the damp smell of rotting wood.

Inside, my father pushed at dark
red boards that gave way softly,
opening out like a spoiling rose.
Finally, there was only a skeleton of timber
and a punctured roof showing sky
against the darkened wood.

He hauled away the leavings
of people we had never known—
newspapers, canning jars, mattresses,
two toilet bowls and a tub—
hooked a cable between the main beam
and the back of the station wagon.

The engine burned, the cable strained,
and the main beam held, and held.
Finally there was a shriek of wood,
the crack of joints pulling undone,
and then a sideways shifting—.
All that summer we cleared away;

my father sorting scrap and siding,
while I pitched dirt against a screen
to sift out glass and nails.
He said he'd build something
smaller with the lumber, and I shifted
soggy boxes to watch centipedes scurrying

through tiny labyrinths of trails.
In long summer evenings after work
he worked. I brought him water
in a thermos, my small hands struggling
to unscrew the lid, pouring water
into the outsized cup. How carefully

I tried to pour: the slow weighted tipping,
then the sudden spill of water,
the way tearing down that barn
seemed to take forever, and now
when I pull on the wide Dutch door
the sliding bolt is rusted shut.

I climb into the empty loft and touch
the wooden crescents
he made to hold my bridles,
the sloping, roof-shaped racks for saddles.
I lie on the floor in a window-square of sun,
watching the suspension of hay dust in air.

The Farriers

I

Mike Boylan had a grumbling brogue and a smoke-colored
    truck with a tin stovepipe in back.
There was always the waiting for him—like a difficult lover,
    he wouldn't commit himself to time.

While he worked, I watched his back through his shirt,
    the white cotton thinned by washing,
translucent with sweat. His forearm was thick as my thigh.
    He smelled of horse and ashes.

Pinching a leg between his leathered knees, he scraped down
    to the blue-gray new horn,
pared away the dead skin of the frog, rasping,
    rounding a hoof into shape.

He held a shoe in blackened tongs, turned it in the stove
    until it glowed, then set it
sizzling on a hoof. After he said it didn't hurt,
    I liked the smell of burning,

the searing of metal and horn. Bending to his work,
    he cursed my horses,
called them *sons of bitches*, even the mares.
    He came from a world where

time was measured by sun and the horses he shod.
    He wandered between stables,
grateful for a breezy day, a steady horse,
    the cold lemonade I'd offer.

II

In memory I see Henry standing square, thick arms
    folded across his chest, watching
a horse move around the ring as if the rhythm
    were a language he could see.

Henry forged shoes that made a horse move differently:
    his bouncing hammer on the anvil
tossed clear notes across the yard; his hands
    moved down a slender leg

tenderly, tapping on crescents of light aluminum—
    dancing shoes, he called them.
The horses moved more freely, jumped higher,
    as if his touch stayed with them.

At lunch he sat in shade with Gunther, his partner,
    eating thick sandwiches
from a box his wife had packed that morning.
    He always worked quietly,

soothing the nervous horses with murmuring sounds
    in a foreign tongue; and because
his words were soft and unintelligible,
    I thought of them as nonsense,

not yet knowing that the words we understand
    can still be incomplete—and only
beginning to learn the precision of a gesture,
    the generous vocabulary of touch.

Not How I Touched It, But That I Touched It At All

As a child I couldn't leave things alone:
a perfect branch must be torn from its crux,
the bark of the black birch peeled back
for wintergreen. When ice began to limn
the shallow puddles, I tested the frost-hatched
covers, pressed my toe against the seam
of water and air. In the pearling fog of early
morning, I waited for the bus, breath-white
billowing, and played at smoking cigarettes,
held damp stems against my lips.

Then the jewelweed rose up. Snapweed,
touch-me-not—I rejected those names—
it longed to be touched. Genus: *impatiens*.
The striated pods grew full and thick,
pale chartreuse and then translucent.
Overnight they grew transparent, revealed
a small, black seed inside, a necessary
dark. When the pods reached their fullness
the lightest pressure caused release.
Over and over, an involuntary gathering
beneath my fingertips: the tangled curls
of filaments arced seeds onto the ground.
Standing in the laden bushes, over and over,
fullness and release. My breath white
in the dark morning, autumn-sharp air.

Social Dancing

The spring I turned twelve
my mother penned my name and
height and age onto a thick
vanilla card, then placed it
in a soft blue envelope
and gave it to me to mail.

Social Dancing, the class was called.
I'd have to wear a dress,
white gloves and party shoes,
dance with sweaty boys
in the chalk-dust gym
on Tuesday afternoons.

I kept the envelope for days,
like a thin blue charm
against my growing up.
First come, first served,
and I'd heard there were always
too many girls.

I thought of my friends—
how their knee socks gave way
to stockings, cotton undershirts
abandoned for shallow cups
against their breasts.
And holding my invitation,

I saw the wooden floor
marked with colored tape,
girls and boys standing
on opposite sides of the gym,
beginning the awkward geometry
of that first box step.

The Narrow Bed

I

First it was my mother's
then it was mine,
the mattress shaped
by our years of slender bodies.
Like a pencil resting
in a desktop groove,
there was only one way
to lie in it. One spring
I brought a young man home.
Guests were not allowed upstairs,
but after my parents left,
we climbed the steps,
past photos mounted
on the stairway wall—
daughters in white blouses,
shiny hair and polished shoes.
He laughed at the bed,
how even for us, unused
to generous spaces,
its solitary width
was too solitary.
Downstairs in daylight
our bodies lit by sun,
the line of his shoulder
over me, my skin dark
against the white rug,
how small and perfect
I seemed to myself then.

II

My father shuffled through the house,
as if lifting a foot
would unbalance him,
air thickened by the scent
of daughters becoming women.
For days he sat in a plastic lawn chair,
gazing over briars
and unmowed grass.
His face went slack;
he would not speak.
We must have seemed
like paper dolls become animate—
we chose black stockings
and bright clothes.
My father dreamed of demure
paper fashions, pressed the tabs
against our backs.
Twenty years before,
fishing in Vermont,
I dropped a sawdust lion
off our perch above the brook.
The bright orange toy
caught between the current and
a branch that spanned the stream.
My father splashed in after it,
rescuing my lion, which dried
slowly and crooked,
the sawdust clumped inside.

But the summer he stared out
over the lawn, the only sound
was ice cubes ticking
in the gin between us.
His daughters would be touched
and touched again.
He would not speak.
He slept curled tight
in my childhood bed.
I couldn't imagine how he'd rest,
shoulders curved against
its narrowness.

March, West Virginia

We lie in your bed looking out across the valley,
the snow is gray as dawn, marked by dark
fence posts, the ridge in the distance
is still a part of night. You tell me
how in summer you lie here to watch
a storm roll over the mountain,
move across the ground, the pouring wall
making the earth dark below its force,
until it comes up to the cabin, where you
have waited for it, to welcome it.
You describe it because you hope
I will be here in summer.
                          After you leave for work,
I can almost hear, on the hill behind me,
the sound of water running under ice.
Sitting in your kitchen, I know this
could be my life. The mountains rise
above the white-clotted valley,
and here in the quiet, I mark this.

Late

That whispered word, inconsequential
until coupled with a woman's voice.
Late, as if the cyclical could ever
be anything but perfect.
I touch myself and the gauzy paper
comes away bloodless, not even

the palest smudge of rose. Like a mirage
I can almost see the colors
of my body's core loosened, the dark
rope of blood unknotting, dropping down.
Sophomore year: driving a friend
to Richmond for an abortion. The red brick

clinic looked like my kindergarten.
The receptionist was kind, the waiting
room bright, and when they took her in
I walked down Linden Street,
past rowhouses and flowerbeds
while they took that small life from her.

I'd learned to drive a stick shift
so I could drive her home.
And waiting now, I'm back
in that October, driving south on 81,
the landscape changing from foothills
to the city's gray mesh, the guardrails

blurring into gray transparence.
I want to go back to these simple
divisions—metal and air—or the year
before they separated girls from boys,
and explained how blood
would come out of each of us.

It seemed unbelievable.
It happened to everyone—my mother,
my teacher, the president's wife!
It would never happen to me.
I wouldn't join the sisterhood
of shadowed conversations, never guessed

that later I would pray for blood
as a farmer prays for rain.
I try to recall which dawn or night,
what failure might have caused this,
and on an afternoon that smells of snow,
a soft, dark turn releasing—.

Provisions

House-sitting in August, I'm asked to pick
the garden, a chicken-wire oval spread
with flattened straw, spotted with yellow
blossoms and red-orange tomatoes.

Warm weight rests in my palm.
I'd forgotten what the fruit itself
smells like: warm earth, mulch and grass,
not like ketchup, tomato sauce, gazpacho.

A year unwinds in slow evasions:
working odd jobs, tending others' gardens,
knowing that movement is temporal relief.
I've come from visiting a friend in the mountains—

neighbors brought her their garden's overflow:
bushels of zucchini and swollen tomatoes.
She had told me their names—Hoot & Olive Dove.
Hoot had dark teeth and a porkpie hat,

Olive wore cat-eyed glasses with pearly frames.
They lived on the shoulder of the mountain
all their lives. We sat on the step, talked about rain,
then they left us to the work of canning—

washing jars, feeding the woodstove, working
toward another season. Jars rattled on the stove,
steam silvered the windows, beads of water
magnified the moon. I thought of their lives,

how long they had lived so close to the weather.
Finishing late, we were full without eating,
two rows of red jars stood on the shelves,
enough to last the winter.

After Fighting

Severn found this place for him—
a willow in the western corner,
rows of cypress dark against the sky.

Graves in a line like hospital beds,
Keats rests near a whitewashed shed
littered with rakes, tin watering cans,

the broken lyre on his stone
not the symbol Severn thought
but Fanny's seal.

The mismatched rhythm of our steps
disturbs the tended gravel path.
Again, we're quiet after fighting.

It is January in Rome, the opacity
of winter sky is light
above the ancient walls. Our damage

unclear and unrelieved by passion.
You wake in mornings curled around
the absence of my shape.

I see from a distance,
down a crowded row of gravestones,
an angel draped across a tomb,

one arm loose against the air;
her wings are large and slack with grief.
Her body reaches forward

as if she had thrown herself
down on a bed, crying, one hand
reaching toward this world.

Emelyn Story, carved by her husband
who followed her death with his own
ten months to the day. Their marriage

lasted longer than Keats' life.
I imagine her husband
picking up his tools again,

tapping his grief into stone,
the careful, chiseled knocking,
hammering back to her youth,

hammering back to that purest
of wanting. I didn't know then
what such love required.

Want

Half-awake, it is now the words can rise
into a stream of breath and sound.
I stretch my legs when no one's looking,

my prickling blood rebellious
at this sitting prayer. At the ashram
the *sunnyasin* wear orange,

loose cotton tunics, floating saris,
wooden beads. Orange of fire
and purification, an earthly reminder

of their vows. Orange to me
is school buses or fingerpaint,
a thick swirl of colors on my hands—

a mixture of the body's red passion,
the benevolence of yellow.
In silence, we're supposed to follow

the simplicity of breath
but I always give in
to the persistence of thought—

I imagine showing you the luna moth,
almost the size of my hand,
which rested at my window,

pale, jade green, with four dusted
eyes on its swallowtail wings.
In the dawn dark sky, a vermilion

edge behind the trees. Mist rises
off the river, which curves wide,
silent at the bottom of the hill.

Easter at Cassis

The narrow road runs high above the water,
turning in from pale cliffs
to run past thinning stone walls.
The hills are white and green with scrub,

the flowers glossy and unfamiliar. We carry
a picnic of yellow and white—
wine and pineapple, bread and cheese—
then lie on sunny ledges high above the sea,

watching families on the hard-pebbled beach
as easy in their nakedness
as we are new in ours.
On Easter Sunday, clattering bells,

the ringing changes pull me toward
a ritual I want to ignore.
I walk through the empty market
to a whitewashed church set against a hill.

Inside, the flowers are bright, unapologetic—
no white lilies, all lush color
and full green. I search the missal
for the words ingrained in another language,

but I can't find my place, so I stop and listen
to the call and response,
the intonation of prayer, to sound
without meaning, softer, more forgiving.

After Daylight Savings

Once I left the clocks on their old time for days,
bartering with abstraction, as if daylight
could be saved, or retrieved by human wish.
I want to accept the lengthening dark,
to take each season as it opens to the next.
Winter is the season I resist.

Winter is the only season I resist,
the sky like dirty milk, the shortened days.
The flight of geese against the whitened light,
their steady pulsing through the sky like a wish
forgotten. The slow descent at dark,
the safety of the marsh, never thinking *where next?*

Always the mind worries on what's next,
His eye is on the sparrow, but I resist
believing I'm included. The mind a field of earth-dark
furrows. I guide myself around a turn each day,
muttering intricate charms, the incantatory wish
against the changing light.

Evening barely lasts in the rapid-falling light,
colors deepen, disappear. I haven't learned the dark's
somber palette, the subtleties of dusk. What I resist
is what I cannot see, and all that's next
comes anyway—it's foolishness to wish
against the shortened day.

Spring forward, fall back. An autumn Sunday
slips into Standard Time. Nothing of the earth resists
the puddles icing over, the trees ash-dark.
Now in this still time the light's
most subtle roots begin, in the quiet before the next
showing, the silence before the wish.

The growing silence before the wish:
wordless, precarious time, as I resist
the fullness of all that's coming next.
There's richness in the sheltering dark,
it shields belief too frail for light,
the brilliance of the coming days.

And light keeps its own counsel, it doesn't resist
or want to know what's coming next. I wish
for light's patience in these days of early dark.

III

What Cheer, Iowa

The What Cheer Bank: half a hexagon in brick
squared off in back where it once fit
against a building now gone, and everywhere else
yard sale signs, pricking lawns like pink flamingos.
We are headed for the fairground where
the dusty track is covered with antique
high chairs, frying pans and rhinestone jewels,
so much left over from our lives.
The ancient Egyptians had the right idea—
bury the household goods with their owner.
I imagine this field a graveyard,
women buried with their Maytag washers,
white enamel corners rising from the earth.
Flea market, from Marché aux Puces, in Paris,
a city distant now, but even Iowa
seems foreign in its way. You search
for a piano stool with a turning wooden seat,
old typewriters distract you—narrow silver legs
like a line of frozen chorus girls.
You must have ten of them already, your letters
buoyant with capitals kicking high above the lines.
At a table piled with tools you touch the planes,
examine blades, and I'm back in early morning,
feeling your palm move over me,
not to smooth the surface, but to know
each curve precisely, to join it perfectly.

High Summer

I walk into the evening
with a chipped china bowl,

barefoot on tilting steps,
the silvered planks

like a crumpled keyboard
spilling down the hill.

Deer move below the house
on currents through the woods,

I follow narrow trails
into a grassy clearing—

a brambled maze of raspberries.
In the blue before night

there's only the doppling of a car
speeding down the road below.

You are away again,
almost at the far point

on the parabola of leaving
and return, while I've come back

to this green stillness.
I touch the fruit

pale against the fading light.
Each hollow cluster

a quilted vessel, a cohesion
of delicate globes

touched with a filament hair.
I brush the fruit from its bending,

allowing my bowl to catch
the soft descent.

The Light Across Three Seasons

All that hasn't yet been said
rises up between us,

and wanting clearer air we climb
a rocky ledge to look out over

the distant fields and silver pines.
Heat and light, water and drought,

the elemental marks us
in increments of dark and light

as tree rings score the weathers
of their growth.

In a room behind a curtain,
a mirror's speckled glass reflects

my summer-shadowed arms.
I've never been so small

as I move against the length of you.
In newness, a feather edge of fear,

the full gravity of desire.
You unlace my shoes, laughing

at the double knots and softly
press me back while the light

behind my eyelids goes orange,
then black.

Later, in half-light, my lips
will find each scar again—

the asphalt smudge on your shoulder,
the pale rain of lines down your back.

My Husband, Planting Roses

Roses won't grow here, the neighbors all say,
but my husband turns the netted earth
and tills a border in the lawn.
Our first anniversary and already we know
each other's predilections—I protest
the expense, the extravagant gesture;
he listens, smiles, does not give in.
The branchy starveling bushes begin blooming
in late spring, but in this year of flooding,
a powdered whiteness coats the leaves
taking back their sheen.
Finally, in August heat, I am out of temper
and idly begin to weed. The lawn is taking back
the ground he claimed, and what I pluck at
as diversion, waiting for the mail,
now becomes specific—aiming at the fescue,
stealing back this stolen space.
Three bushes of the twelve have died,
their branches blackened, waxy-ended,
but the others start to bloom again.
I've made this mistake before—
expecting beauty to be fragile, underestimating
the persistence of luxuriance and color.

At the Genetics Counselor

The clinical fluorescence allows no room
for softer light or shadow.

A glass of water trembles on the table.

The notebook displays disorderly chromosomes:
the proliferate migration of pairs

like a marching band gone awry,
an extra column in silent practice

changing the symmetry of the whole.

We must chart our family histories,
make a tree of missing branches.

What happened to your Aunt Rhea?
A blackjack dealer in Reno,

the last my husband heard.

Peasant Irish on both sides, I believed
myself a sturdy transplant.

And when she calls with bad news,

something very rare, something worse
than we imagine, the teacups rattle

on the shelf and branches knock
against the house.

The summer leaves turn silver,
as if awaiting rain.

Church Hall Rummage Sale

Paisley shirts with pointed collars,
chunk-heeled sandals, unwelcome toys—

I stop for pie with latticed crust,
children selling lemonade.

A walleyed man with a crucifix
touches a musical jewelry box—

the plastic ballerina will not turn
on her velvet ledge. A mirror holds

her frozen pirouette. I touch
a corset whose form I couldn't fill,

its lengthened ribs and jutting cups
an ample woman's shape. I imagine

swelling flesh above the girded sides,
like warm bread rising

past the lip of a pan, a woman
who knew the secrets of laughter

and long marriage. A dogwood blooms
in the open window, white petals open

like a palm raised in prayer. Once I believed
in lives more simple than mine.

Spectator

Each summer my sisters raced, arms
pulling through the lapidary blue.

They couldn't hear my cheering:
caps crowning the water, slick backs

breaking surface. From above,
I never saw them turn: the kick

and tuck, the push from the wall,
the way this child pushed from me,

making its small flipturn inside
my body, as I hovered above

its salty element, breathing, sliding
through the summer air.

Fallibility

Growing by the road in marshy hollows,
the moss-soft flowers seem autumn's
diminished answer to the flocks
of August lilies—pale orange, saffron—
swaying by the roadside until scythed
by late summer, leaving them corpselike,
closed upon the ground.

Not grief, but the summer light just after.
In the rich damp of autumn, the cusp of
possibility, a cup of tea, an unexpected kiss.
The marsh birds feed among the cattails
then dive into the cold. I wait for rain
on the roof, the divine collapse revealing
some symmetry or plan.

Five Elements

Fire

Expecting the comfort of ashes, of reduction by heat,
his body seemed intransigent. Pallid clay
nested in the casket, satin heart of the room.
My sister wanted water, child at her breast,
and I moved through rooms of silk and paisley,
hounds-tooth, gold. No cups but flowers, their fluted
throats too small to hold a dram of water.
My sister's tongue is silver, the bitter burned away.
Summer burned outside, and I wanted it let in.

Water

Flanges in my ear, invisible tide: cochlea,
canals, small salty bones. The horizon tilts
and levels, the compass quivers and floats
in the brine. The snow's bright plumage gathers
on the sill. My son swirls maps in crayon,
navigates by crimson sun. We plant kidney beans
in paper cups. We spin colored yarn on sticks.
I lie on the floor to still the turning world.
My small son turns in my arms.

Metal

When metal collapses it is fixed in the mind,
a gnomon rising in the dry, white space.
I eat bitter greens, keep my eyes on the east.
Wind sieves me clean in the minted cold,
circles of marsh grass bracelet my wrists.
We are not yet at harvest. *I will lie down
beside you. I shall lie down beside.*
The cattails leaking fluff like discarded toys.
We are learning the nature of grief.

Wood

The baby born face down, the mother screams.
Billy goats rattle the old wooden bridge.
The rectangular dark of the goats' copper eyes,
tiny hooves, sour jaws, all sinew and bone.
Only for the bold is there safety far from home.
No sweet without risk.
A mother marked by cautionary tales—
La Petite Chèvre de Monsieur Seguin.
The baby born fist pressed against his cheek.

Earth

The mouth is filled with yellow flowers, fragrance
of cut grass. My son is learning to sing rounds,
disdaining the notion of a finger to his ear.
The better to hear you with, my dear.
We fill our mouths with faltering thirds, but he slips
into my part. No music without movement,
no sound without vibration. Friction of horsehair
catgut and wire. He draws the bow across. I tell him
Listen to your part, and I will follow.

The Frail Harmonic

I can't hear myself think, my mother would say,
and I'm sure it was true—four daughters
who prattled and bickered and sang—
though I couldn't imagine the sound of her thought,
or what space of quiet she required.
I sang in the car, sang in my room,
believing I'd find the trick
for singing harmony with myself:
that my throat could open
to sound in perfect thirds—
pitchpipe, harmonica, thrum in the chest.

                              Moored in the body
the soul hovers in the breath, our inconstant
motion toward an unheard melody.
Monks chanting toward a sacred sound
practice for years to achieve a doubled pitch.
Their cavernous ground notes
echoing the earth's fierce center,
and above the rolling syllables a piercing
overtone, tethered to the earthly drum.

In unexpected solitude I am quiet in our house.
Words rise up against the silence of the page.
Shadows move on the wooden table, evidence of wind.
I'm passing through my mother's shadow—
she makes a settling motion, pressing down the air.

                          In summer's hovering quiet
before the starting of September life,
there is a spaciousness of mind, a sense of
listening in the silence, or not listening
but knowing, the still song of *I am*,
and touching with the mind's profusion
the delicate gap between this world and the elusive one,
the one that waits for our attention.

Acknowledgments

A number of these poems first appeared, in slightly different versions, in two chapbooks: *In The Blue Before Night*, published by Heatherstone Press in 1993, and *Sure Knowledge*, published by Parallel Press in 1999. My thanks to Jeanne Braham, Ken Frazier, Andrea Potos, and Tracy Honn.

Thanks also to the editors of the magazines in which these individual poems first appeared:

The Atlanta Review	"The Cost"
Billee Murray Denny Awards	"Labor," under the title "The Barn"
The Connecticut Review	"At the Church Hall Rummage Sale"
Gargoyle	"Five Elements"
The Georgia Review	"Belleek"
literary hot girls review	"Late"
The Montserrat Review	"The Silver Screen," "Elegy"
Nerve.com	"Not How I Touched It, But That I Touched It At All"
Organica	"March, West Virginia"
Poet Lore	"High Summer"
Poetry Ireland Review	"Elegy"
Prairie Schooner	"Quiet After Fighting," "The Frail Harmonic"
Red Dragonfly Press	"The Discovery of Wine"
Shenandoah	"For My Father, On My Sister's Wedding Day"
South Coast Poetry Journal	"The Warmth of Blue Glass"
South Florida Poetry Review	"Social Dancing"
Sunrust	"Provisions"
What Light	"Water That Feeds the Battenkill River"

"Fallibility," "At the Genetics Counselor," "Spectator," "The Discovery of Wine," and "The Light Across Three Seasons" appeared in a limited fine press edition, *Fallibility,* by Sutton Hoo Press. Thanks to CMO.

"Belleek" was reprinted in the anthology *To Sing Along the Way: Minnesota Women Poets from Pre-Territorial Days to the Present,* edited by Joyce Sutphen, Thom Tammaro, and Connie Wanek, New Rivers Press, 2006.

"At the Genetics Counselor" was reprinted in the anthology *Encore: More of Parallel Press Poets,* published by the University of Wisconsin-Madison, 2006.

"Belleek" and "Elegy" were reprinted in the anthology *The Book of Irish American Poetry from the Eighteenth Century to the Present,* edited by Daniel Tobin and published by University of Notre Dame Press, 2007.

"After Daylight Savings" appeared as "Sestina After Daylight Savings" in *The Watershed Anthology,* edited by Chad Oness and published by the University

Biography

Elizabeth Oness's poems and stories have appeared in *The Hudson Review*, *Shenandoah*, *Glimmer Train*, *The Georgia Review*, *The Gettysburg Review*, and other literary magazines. She has published two chapbooks of poems, *In the Blue Before Night* (Heatherstone Press) and *Sure Knowledge* (Parallel Press). Her stories have received an O. Henry Prize, a Nelson Algren Award, and other commendations. Her short story collection, *Articles of Faith*, won the 2000 Iowa Short Fiction Prize, and her first novel, *Departures*, was published by Penguin in 2004. *Twelve Rivers of the Body* won the 2007 Gival Press Novel Award, and was published in 2008. Oness is an associate professor of English at Winona State University and directs marketing and development for Sutton Hoo Press, a literary fine press. She lives with her family in rural Minnesota.